SINESS LEADERS AND THE PRESS PRAISE

STRATEGIC SELLING™

A practical guide offering new insight into the way salesmen can successfully promote big-ticket items to large organizations."

—*Financial Post*

"Strategic Selling is in a class by itself. . . . We use it to plan all our national account sales."

—**Jack Schang, Chairman and CEO, Ryder/P.I.E. Nationwide, Inc.**

"We use Strategic Selling as a means of substituting analysis for guesswork . . . and for reviewing and following up on major sales."

—**Lowell E. Gutzler, VP and General Manager, Marriott Corporation**

"Thanks to Bob and Steve's conceptual approach to complex sales, we're now a major carrier in the [group life and health] field."

—**William J. Burton, VP, Group Life and Health Sales, Massachusetts Mutual Life Insurance Company**

"A totally professional planning process. If Willy Loman had taken the Miller Heiman program, he'd have been salesman of the year."

—**Walter H. Drew, Senior VP and General Sales Manager, Kimberly-Clark Corporation, Consumer Products Division**

"Miller Heiman's Strategic Selling course provides an effective process for selling our company's products and services which our bankers find invaluable. . . . We have been delighted."

—**William R. Caldwell, EVP, and COO, The Bank of California, N.A.**

"A method that sales professionals can use effectively. The authors clearly and engagingly describe numerous 'workshops,' in which readers can apply what they have just read to their own sales experiences. Professionally yet clearly presented."

—*ALA Booklist*

Robert B. Miller rose from associate to vice-president-general manager for North American operations at Kepner-Tregoe, Inc., which offers consulting services for senior management of Fortune 500 corporations and the federal and state governments. He personally consulted with such companies as Ford, General Motors, Citicorp, and Rolls-Royce. In 1974, he founded Robert B. Miller & Associates, where he began developing the innovative sales systems and other programs that have made Miller Heiman & Associates one of America's top sales consulting firms.

Stephen E. Heiman rose in nineteen years from national account salesman for IBM (where he increased sales in all product areas by more than 35 percent and was in the top 5 percent for total sales and percentage quota) to director of marketing at Kepner-Tregoe, to executive vice-president of North American Van Lines, where he increased sales and profits by 36 percent in four years. In 1978, he joined Robert Miller as co-principal and full partner in what became Miller Heiman & Associates Inc. and has since helped train thousands of sales management executives from top corporations across the country.

STRATEGIC SELLING℠

The Unique Sales System Proven Successful by America's Best Companies

Robert B. Miller
Stephen E. Heiman
with Tad Tuleja

WARNER BOOKS

A Time Warner Company

STRATEGIC SELLING^{SM} is a Service Mark of Miller Heiman Inc., 1595 Meadow Wood Lane, Suite 2, Reno, NV 89502.

Warner Books Edition

This Warner Books edition is published by arrangement with William Morrow and Company, 105 Madison Avenue, New York, New York 10016.

Warner Books, Inc., 1271 Avenue of the Americas, New York, NY 10020

A Time Warner Company

Printed in the United States of America

First Warner Books Printing: March 1986

20 19 18 17 16 15 14

Book design by Patty Lowy

Library of Congress Cataloging-in-Publication Data

Miller, Robert B. (Robert Bruce), 1931–
    Strategic selling.

    Reprint. Originally published: New York: Morrow, 1985.
    Includes index.
    1. Selling. I. Heiman, Stephen E. II. Tuleja, Tad, 1944–   . III. Title.
[HF5438.25.M567   1985b]   658.8'1   85-26566

FOREWORD

When Strategic Selling was first introduced to us at Hewlett-Packard some eight years ago, the concept had an immediate appeal. It was an approach to selling that represented the high degree of professionalism and the kind of buyer-seller relationship to which we aspired. Thousands of HP sales engineers worldwide have been trained in Strategic Selling, and its influence can be directly seen in the results they have attained.

Strategic Selling doesn't attempt to teach the sales representative how to make an effective pitch. It doesn't rely on luck or charisma. And most importantly from our perspective, Strategic Selling is not manipulation.

The methodology in this book looks at the buying decision. The focus is outward, on the customers we serve. Their needs—both organizational and personal—are identified. The resultant analysis allows us to better determine how we can add value to that customer's organization and create a long-term business relationship that benefits all parties. Strategic Selling points not only outward to customers, but forward. It aims at creating the kinds of partnerships that will last over the years to come.

Strategic Selling has strengthened Hewlett-Packard's customer focus by providing a common discipline and vocabulary that have helped create a unified customer emphasis throughout the company. Our sales representatives have found it immediately applicable to the accounts they serve. Its usefulness has spanned product disciplines and national boundaries.

Considered a somewhat revolutionary approach when first introduced, Strategic Selling has also spanned the years very well. This is because the objectives it seeks—providing customers with real value and establishing long-term relationships with them—are timeless. Professionals seeking those goals will find this volume a most useful resource.

—JOHN A. YOUNG, President and
Chief Executive Officer,
Hewlett-Packard Company